the

TRUE SAINT
NICHOLAS

the
TRUE SAINT
NICHOLAS

Why He Matters to Christmas

❄ ❄ ❄

William J. Bennett

HOWARD BOOKS
A DIVISION OF SIMON & SCHUSTER, INC.

NEW YORK · NASHVILLE · LONDON · TORONTO · SYDNEY

Published by Howard Books, a division of Simon & Schuster, Inc.
1230 Avenue of the Americas, New York, NY 10020
www.howardpublishing.com

The True Saint Nicholas © 2009 William J. Bennett

Library of Congress Cataloging-in-Publication Data is available.

978-1-4165-6746-2

10 9 8 7 6 5 4 3 2 1

HOWARD and colophon are registered trademarks
of Simon & Schuster, Inc.

Manufactured in the United States of America
For information regarding special discounts for bulk purchases,
please contact: Simon & Schuster Special Sales at
1-800-456-6798 or business@simonandschuster.com.

The Simon & Schuster Speakers Bureau can bring authors
to your live event. For more information or to book an event,
contact the Simon & Schuster Speakers Bureau at
1-866-248-3049 or visit our website at www.simonspeakers.com.

Edited by Denny Boultinghouse and Susan Wilson
Cover design by Mark Summers
Interior design by Jaime Putorti
Photography/illustrations: Page 5: © DeA Picture Library / Art Resource
Page 43: Don Lorenzo Monaco
The compilation copyright is held by Zenodot Verlagsgesellschaft mbH and
licensed under the GNU Free Documentation License.
Page 79: Thomas Nast, public domain.

This book is dedicated to all the children
who have cherished the name "Saint Nicholas,"
in hopes that his story will deepen their affection.

CONTENTS

....

....

ACKNOWLEDGMENTS

....

I am indebted to friends, colleagues, and loved ones who, in the spirit of Saint Nicholas, have devoted their talents and encouragement to make this book possible.

John Cribb helped me peer through the mists of time and flesh out the story of Nicholas.

Seth Leibsohn gave his always dependable and wise advice.

Noreen Burns was an early advocate of this project and helped keep things moving smoothly from start to finish.

Matt Jacobson suggested the idea of a book about Nicholas and kept after me until I finally did it.

Denny Boultinghouse of Howard Books shepherded the book along as good editors do. He is a gentleman.

....

Bob Barnett, my longtime agent to whom I always listen, because he knows what he is talking about, once again made the deal that made this book possible.

My wife, Elayne, stays up long after I have gone to bed, working on matters large and small, from saving children to getting book titles (like this one) just right. I am always grateful to her and to our sons, John and Joe, for their support. They are my greatest blessings.

When most of us hear the name "Saint Nicholas," we immediately think of Santa Claus. As children, we listened wide-eyed to Clement Clarke Moore's famous poem about the night before Christmas, when "down the chimney St. Nicholas came with a bound." At some point along the way, we may have asked an older and wiser acquaintance why Santa sometimes goes by this alias. The answer we received was probably not very informative. And once we are all grown up, with children of our own, and by chance are asked the same question, we still are not sure. If pressed, we might guess that there was once a very good man named Nicholas, and his name somehow came to be connected with

Santa Claus. But Saint Nicholas remains an elusive figure to us.

He is elusive even to scholars who study such matters. They believe that Saint Nicholas served as a bishop during the fourth century in the town of Myra, on the coast of the eastern Mediterranean Sea. He may have attended the famous Council of Nicaea convened by Constantine the Great in 325 to resolve issues troubling the Christian Church. But the details of his life and work remain sketchy. If he wrote anything, it is long gone. The first known Nicholas "biography" dates to the eighth or ninth century, long after his death, when a Greek monk known as Michael the Archimandrite assembled a collection of tales about him.

We are left to piece together his life as best we can, using what we know and a good bit of surmise to arrive at the most likely story. Often we must rely on tradition as well as clues provided by the history of the times in which he lived. If the reputation he left behind means anything, we know there was something remarkable about this holy man. For hundreds of years, his name has been invoked, his deeds recounted. His shadow falls across epochs.

Why bother with the history of Saint Nicholas? For one thing, his is a fascinating story. Its sheer vastness of scale is astounding. It stretches from the crossroads of Europe,

Asia, and Africa to the Americas and beyond. It crosses oceans, deserts, and frozen arctic climes. This is an adventure tale complete with emperors, knights, villains, shipwrecks, kidnappings, treasure, and dark dungeons. It is the age-old struggle of good against evil, of right against might.

But there is a larger reason to remember Saint Nicholas: He matters to Christmas. This saintly man who lived so long ago has come to influence one of our holiest seasons and most beloved holidays. This influence that has come across so many centuries is a kind of miracle. It is evidence of God's love.

One purpose of this book is to help put Saint Nicholas back into Christmas. It explains his connection with Santa Claus, and the common spirit they share. As you will see, Saint Nicholas makes Santa Claus a larger and richer figure than you might expect him to be.

So here is the story of Nicholas, based on what we can reasonably conjecture. It is a story worth knowing. I hope that once you know it, you will remember Saint Nicholas each December. You may never again think of Santa Claus in quite the same way. If that is the case, then this book will have achieved its aim of helping to deepen the spirit of Christmas.

part one

❄

LIFE OF
NICHOLAS

....

CHAPTER ONE

Answered Prayers and Secret Alms

*L*ike many good things, this story begins with a mother's prayer.

During the days of the Roman Empire, in a province called Lycia, in what is now the country of Turkey, a husband and wife longed for a child. Theophanes and Nonna, their names are said to have been. Their home was Patara, a flourishing town at the mouth of the river Xanthos on the Mediterranean coast, a place where the forested hills sloped down to the clear blue sea.

Theophanes and Nonna were a well-to-do couple. Perhaps they inherited land and money. Theophanes may have run a prosperous trade in cloth or milled grains. History does not tell us. We know only that, according to one old chronicle, they were people "of substantial lineage, holding property enough without superfluity."

Their comfortable lives were troubled by one great unhappiness: though they had been married for many years, they had never managed to have children. As time passed, they wept and waited, but no child came. Still, Nonna refused to give up hope. Instead, she did something very wise. She prayed. Like Hannah in the First Book of Samuel in the Bible, she poured out her soul to God, asking him to remember her.

It must have seemed like a miracle when late in life, after so many hopes and tears, Nonna's prayer was answered around the year A.D. 280 with the birth of a son. She surely recalled how Hannah, who was finally blessed with the boy Samuel, had vowed to "give him unto the Lord all the days of his life" (1 Samuel 1:11 KJV).

Some say that when Nonna's child was placed in his bath right after birth, he stood up by himself and raised his arms as if in praise of God. Others say that on Wednesdays and Fridays, traditional days of fasting for early Christians, he refused to nurse until after sundown. Such are the legends. But there must have been something that made the proud parents hope that their child would someday serve

God and his fellow men in some remarkable way. They christened the baby Nicholas, a name that in Greek means "people's victor," after an uncle who was an abbot at a nearby monastery.

Patara was a good town to grow up in, a bustling center of trade full of sights for a boy to explore. Wide avenues lined with columns and paved with stones led from town gates past houses, shops, and temples to busy agorai (market squares). Beneath brightly colored awnings, merchants arranged their goods: grapes, olives, cheese, herbs, dyed wool and cotton, pottery, jewelry, leather, glassware, skins of wine. The shoppers who haggled with vendors and the men who swapped news in the shade of roofed colonnades all spoke Greek, the dominant language of that part of the world. Young Nicholas must have spent many hours listening to the shouts of the tradesmen advertising their wares and the talk of women filling jugs with water at the public fountains.

As he roamed the streets of Patara, the boy saw reminders of both his proud Greek heritage and imperial Rome's wide reach. A temple to Apollo drew travelers hoping to divine the future from a revered oracle. The grand assembly building, where officials from all over Lycia met to debate, could seat one thousand people. Elegant baths with rooms covered by marble tiles dotted the city. A massive monument with three Roman arches, built to honor a governor of Lycia, supported an aqueduct that brought water to Patara's inhabitants.

On a hillside near the sea stood the favorite spot of many Patarans, the amphitheater. More than two dozen tiers of stone seats rose above a raised stage where actors spoke or sang their lines. The crowds that gathered to enjoy comedies, tragedies, and dances could be a rowdy bunch, stomping their feet when pleased or throwing olive pits when disappointed by the show.

But Nicholas's favorite spot may well have been the port, where the boy could watch fishing boats unload the day's catch and merchants' ships arrive from points around the eastern Mediterranean: Rhodes, Cyprus, Antioch, Alexandria, and beyond. Occasionally seaman who had made it as far as Rome itself sailed into Patara. They brought news of Roman armies on the march, edicts of emperors, and tales of distant places like North Africa and Gaul.

* * *

AT ABOUT AGE SEVEN, Nicholas was placed under the charge of a pedagogue, a trusted slave who took him to school, helped him with lessons, and kept him out of mischief. The boy gathered with other students under a roofed colonnade to study grammar and arithmetic. He practiced writing with a stylus on a wooden tablet covered with beeswax, and listened intently as the schoolmaster told ancient stories such as how Achilles killed Hector outside the walls of Troy.

But there was one part of the boy's education not to be trusted to a pedagogue or schoolmaster, and that was the matter of faith. Theophanes and Nonna had embraced a new and growing religion, one that required utmost devotion. They were members of Patara's Christian community.

In the two and a half centuries since the time of Jesus, Christianity had spread from the remote province of Judea on the eastern Mediterranean to much of the Roman Empire. The story of the carpenter from Galilee had won converts from Palestine to Britain. His message of love brought new hope to believers. Christianity welcomed all races and classes into a community that offered refuge in a tempest-tossed world.

On Sundays, Nicholas and his parents attended services in a neighbor's house, where they prayed, sang hymns, and studied scripture. They loved the Book of Psalms for its soul-stirring verses, such as, "Make a joyful noise unto the

Lord, all ye lands. Serve the Lord with gladness: come before his presence with singing" (Psalm 100:1–2 KJV). They carefully memorized the words of Jesus: "Inasmuch as ye have done it unto one of the least of these my brethren, ye have done it unto me" (Matthew 25:40 KJV). They shared bread and wine in remembrance of the Last Supper so they would be one with Christ. At the end of prayers they said *Amen* (so be it), and they sounded praise with the word *Alleluia* (God be praised).

Nicholas loved hearing stories about the boy David slaying the giant Goliath, Daniel standing unharmed in the pit of hungry lions, and the friends of the paralyzed man lowering him through the roof of a crowded house so Jesus might heal him. He learned that the Apostle Paul, traveling on the road to Damascus, was struck down by a blinding light and heard a voice saying, "Saul, Saul, why do you persecute me?" The tireless missionary had visited Patara on one of his famous journeys and left behind a small group of converts. Christians copied the letters that Paul wrote to congregations in places such as Corinth, Galatia, and Philippi, and passed them from church to church, pouring over words such as, "[Love] bears all things, believes all things, hopes all things, endures all things" (1 Corinthians 13:7 NASB).

Nicholas's parents taught him early on that Christians served God by serving the less fortunate. In an age when the general rule of existence was "Fend for yourself or die," a Christian's duty was to help others. Churches organized to care for the poor and sick. "See how those Christians love one another!" pagans marveled.

At times it was dangerous to be a Christian. The Roman Empire, though vast and mighty, faced desperate problems: a series of weak emperors, outbreaks of plague, generals who fought each other for power, attacks by barbarians along the empire's borders. When officials needed scapegoats to take the brunt of public frustrations, it was all too easy to single out Christians who refused to worship the old gods of Rome and sacrifice to the emperor.

The boy Nicholas heard stories of how the emperor Nero had blamed Christians for a disastrous fire that swept Rome in A.D. 64, and how he had made human torches of Christians to light his garden at night. He heard about Polycarp, bishop of Smyrna in Asia Minor, who was seized by the proconsul Statius Quadratus and ordered to curse Christ.

"I have wild beasts," the proconsul threatened. "If you do not repent, I will have you thrown to them."

"Send for them," Polycarp replied.

"If you do not despise the wild beasts, I will order you to be burned alive."

"Why do you delay? Bring on what you will."

They burned him alive while the crowd shouted, "This is the father of the Christians! This is the destroyer of our gods!"

In times of persecution, Christians might live one edict away from imprisonment or death. In years when rulers let them alone, they remained a close-knit community, protective of each other and wary of rumors of official displeasure.

But if being a Christian brought occasional scorn or danger, it also brought immeasurable rewards. As Nicholas grew, his faith grew. The old writers tell us that he began to spend less time following boyish pursuits, and more time pondering the message that Jesus had brought to the world. As he approached manhood, he discovered that the fruit of the Spirit is love, joy, and peace.

✳   ✳   ✳

THEN SOMETHING HAPPENED THAT surely must have tested his faith: a plague swept through Lycia, passing from town to town, cutting down whole families, striking rich and poor alike. Theophanes and Nonna were among the dead.

Nicholas, left alone in the world, went to live with his uncle at the monastery to recover from the blow. Slowly, bewilderment and despair gave way to acceptance. He asked God for strength and discovered that it came to him. As he healed, he resolved to train for the priesthood. As a first step, he made up his mind to give away his possessions, including the inheritance left to him by his parents. This decision gave rise to the most beloved story about Nicholas.

In Patara, there lived a family that had fallen on hard times. They had once been wealthy, but misfortunes had overtaken them, and now they were so poor they had barely enough to live on. The father had tried to find work, but when people saw his soft hands, which had never known any kind of hard labor, they took him to be lazy, and turned him away.

The man had three daughters of marriageable age, but their chances of finding husbands were grim since the father could offer no dowries. (In those days, a young woman needed a dowry to attract an offer of marriage.) As their financial situation grew desperate, the father realized that the only way to ensure the survival of his children was to sell them into servitude. At least that way they would have enough to eat.

When news of the family's plight reached Nicholas, he at once set about thinking of a way to help them. He remembered Jesus' teaching that "when you give to the poor, do not let your left hand know what your right hand is doing, so that your giving will be in secret" (Matthew 6:3–4 NASB). He soon came up with a plan. That night, he put several gold coins into a small bag and started out for the home of the father and his three daughters.

The hour was late and the streets deserted when he arrived. Inside the house, the family was sleeping. Nicholas crept up to a window, reached through, and dropped the bag of gold. (Some say that it landed in a shoe, others in a stocking that had been left hanging to dry.) Then he hurried away before anyone saw him.

The next morning the family discovered the bag of gold. Weeping with joy and astonishment, they fell to their knees to thank God for the generous gift. Not only did they have money to live on for some time, there was enough to provide a generous dowry for the oldest daughter, and she was soon married.

When Nicholas saw how much happiness his secret gift had caused, he decided the second daughter must have a dowry, too. He went to the house at night, as before, and dropped a second bag through the window. The next morning brought more tears of joy and astonishment, and more thanks to God for the miraculous gift. The second daughter soon had her dowry and was married.

The father dared to hope that his third daughter would also receive a gift that would allow her to marry. But now he was determined to find out who the earthly angel who had saved them might be. Night after night he stayed up, waiting and watching. Finally, late one night, just as he had concluded that their mysterious benefactor had deserted them, a bag of gold came flying through the window.

The man rushed out of the house, ran after the shadowy figure that was hurrying away, and caught it by the cloak. When he recognized Nicholas, he fell to his knees and began to kiss the hands that had helped his family so graciously. Nicholas asked him to stand, and told him to thank God instead. He begged the father not to tell anyone the secret of who had left the gold.

Despite his longing for anonymity, Nicholas's act of generosity set him on the path to becoming the world's most famous gift giver.

CHAPTER TWO

One Whom the Lord Called to Him

Nicholas plunged into his training for the priesthood. Gone now were any luxuries he had known as a boy. He fasted often and slept on the floor in order to focus his thoughts on the task ahead.

His uncle offered patient guidance, putting into his hands precious manuscripts to study. In the Book of Acts, Nicholas read how the apostles first spread the news about Jesus, how on the day of the Pentecost they heard the sound of a rushing wind and saw tongues of fire, and how they began to speak in tongues. He poured over Peter's first sermon, memorizing words such as, "For the promise is to you and to your children and to all that are far off, every one whom the Lord our God calls to him" (Acts 2:39 RSV).

He studied the *Didache*, a manual for Christian living and worship. It outlined the roles of bishops, priests, and deacons, as well as rules for baptism, Communion, penance, and fasting. From the *Didache* he learned one of the oldest prayers for the Eucharist: "As this broken bread was scattered over the hills, but was gathered together and made one, so let your church be gathered together from the ends of the earth into your kingdom."

He searched the writings of early Christian leaders for wisdom. "Here is the beginning and the end of life," Ignatius of Antioch had written. "Faith is the beginning, the end is love." In the epistles of Clement of Rome he found models for sermons: "Day and night show to us the resurrection; the night is lulled to rest, the day ariseth; the day departeth, the night cometh on."

Tradition says that Nicholas decided to follow the example of his uncle and make a trip to the Holy Land. He boarded an Egyptian merchant vessel that sailed east along the coast of Asia Minor, rounded the island of Cyprus, and continued south along the coast of Palestine, stopping along the way at port cities such as Sidon and Tyre. He arrived at the harbor of Caesarea, famous for its ingenious concrete sea wall, then joined a caravan for the overland journey to Jerusalem.

At that time, around the year 300, Jerusalem was a city under Roman occupation. Much of the old city that Jesus knew had been destroyed and buried beneath Roman construction. But Jerusalem's Christian community welcomed pilgrims such as Nicholas, sheltered them, and guided them to holy sites. Nicholas followed in Jesus' footsteps. He visited the room of the Last Supper, where Jesus last shared bread and wine with his disciples; Golgotha, where Jesus was crucified; and the place of the Holy Sepulcher, where his body had been laid. Nicholas also journeyed to Bethlehem, and it is said that he slept in a cave not unlike the grotto where tradition says the baby Jesus was born.

When the time came to go home, Nicholas returned to Caesarea and struck a bargain with the captain of a merchant vessel to drop him off in Patara. On such journeys, passengers had no cabins or beds. They had to content themselves with a spot on deck amid the stacks and piles of cargo. The ship set out with a fair wind. Nicholas passed the time by chatting with the seamen and gazing at the passing coastline.

Then the weather changed. A storm blew out of nowhere, lashing the boat with fierce gales, and waves crashed over the bow. As the winds howled, Nicholas no doubt thought of the storm that overwhelmed the ship carrying Paul to Rome for trial. The Book of Acts tells how Paul watched the desperate sailors try to save the vessel: "As we were violently storm-tossed, they began next day to throw the cargo overboard; and the third day they cast out with their own hands the tackle of the ship. And when neither sun nor stars appeared for many a day, and no small tempest lay on us, all hope of our being saved was at last abandoned" (Acts 27:18–20 RSV).

Nicholas tried to calm the mariners with prayers for deliverance. When the storm finally subsided, they were still afloat, but they discovered that the rudder had been smashed. They drifted for days with no land in sight, until the sailors gave up hope of any fate except dying of thirst on the open sea.

Nicholas refused to give in to despair. One morning as the crew woke, one of them gave a shout. There, on the horizon, lay the coast. The winds and currents pushed them steadily toward land, and as they drew near they were astonished to realize that they had drifted to Patara.

THE DAY CAME WHEN Nicholas completed his religious training, and his proud uncle ordained him as a priest. "Blessed is the flock that will be worthy to have him as its pastor," his uncle told the Christian community of Patara, "because this one will shepherd well the souls of those who have gone astray, will nourish them on the pasturage of piety, and will be a merciful helper in misfortune and tribulation."

Nicholas took up the hard, endless work of the ministry. "From the minute he became a priest, one can hardly keep count of the virtue and goodness he spread about him, of the nights spent at his devotions, days of fasting, steadfast good will, and his prayers for all," reports Symeon Metaphrastes, who compiled stories of Nicholas hundreds of years after his death.

In every avenue and agora in Patara, Nicholas found opportunities to do God's will, whether that meant simply offering a kind word to a stranger, settling a dispute between friends, or convincing neighbor to help neighbor. Whenever he passed the house where he had left three bags of gold, he smiled to himself.

As he worked, he did his best to live up to the qualities that Polycarp of Smyrna had laid down for clergy in the second century in his letter to the Philippians: "And let the presbyters [priests] be compassionate and merciful to all, bringing back those that wander, visiting all the sick, and not neglecting the widow, the orphan, or the poor, but always 'providing for that which is becoming in the sight of God and man'; abstaining from all wrath . . . and unjust judgment; keeping far off from all covetousness, not quickly crediting [an evil report] against any one, not severe in judgment, as knowing that we are all under a debt of sin."

The years passed quickly, and Nicholas's reputation for kindness and generosity spread. The Christian community in Patara grew. "As people observed his goodness, many followed his example and teachings," Symeon Metaphrastes says. "They scorned a material, transient existence and placed their trust in the eternal."

Eventually Nicholas's dedication led to a promotion and high honor. He was chosen to be bishop of Myra, an important city several miles east of Patara on the Lycian coast.

There is an old, strange story about how Nicholas became bishop. The man who had served as the bishop of Myra for many years had died, and the other bishops of the region gathered in the city to elect someone to succeed him. They discussed the matter for several days, and prayed over it, but reached no agreement over who would be the right choice. Finally one of the oldest and wisest bishops stood and suggested that they should put the matter into God's hands. He announced that he had had a dream in which a voice told him to watch the doors of the church before morning prayers. The first person named Nicholas to enter the church would be the man they were looking for.

Would the bishops be willing to try it? They would. As the time for the morning prayer service approached, the old bishop stationed himself near the church door and waited.

Meanwhile, Nicholas, in town to pay his respects to the memory of the deceased bishop, had awakened at dawn. Dressing quickly, he headed to church to spend some time in quiet meditation before the prayer service began. As he stepped through the door, an old bishop he did not know stopped him.

"What do people call you, my son?" the old man asked.

"My name is Nicholas, your servant," he answered with humility.

"Follow me, child."

Taking him by the hand, he led him before the other

bishops and cried, "Here, my brothers, is Nicholas. Let us greet our new bishop."

The bewildered Nicholas at first refused the appointment, insisting that he wasn't ready for such responsibility. But it is a difficult thing to say no to a room full of bishops, and he finally accepted.

Did it really happen that way? No one knows. Certainly, in those days people put much more stock in dreams and visions than we do today. They often looked for signs from God to help them reach a decision. Congregations sometimes chose leaders by lottery as a way to determine God's will. In any event, Nicholas became leader of the Christian community in Myra.

❋　❋　❋

THE YOUNG BISHOP HAD barely settled into his new role when he met the greatest test of his life. The tragedy known as the Great Persecution fell upon the Christian Church.

It came at a time when the Roman Empire was under enormous strain. Enemies constantly launched attacks on the empire's borders: Goths, Saxons, and Franks in the north, Persians in the east, Moors in the south. In Rome itself, the rule of law often disappeared amid riots and drunken brawls.

Diocletian, who became emperor in A.D. 284, was determined to bring order to chaos. A man who expected his commands to be followed without delay, he grew suspicious of Christians who refused to worship the old gods of Rome or sacrifice to the emperor. His heir apparent, Galerius, harbored stronger hatreds. He was convinced that Christians were enemies of the state.

At a sacrifice attended by the two rulers, the imperial priests had trouble reading the usual signs on the livers of sacrificed beasts. They slaughtered animal after animal, to no avail. Then someone noticed that Christians present during the ceremony had made the sign of the cross. Their meddling had interfered with the divinations, the imperial priests complained.

Egged on by Galerius, Diocletian flew into a rage. In A.D. 303, he decreed that Christian churches were to be destroyed, services banned, and scriptures burned. Christians could no longer hold public office. Further edicts brought the arrest of Christian leaders and an order that all Christians sacrifice to pagan gods.

Years of terror followed. Christians who did not submit faced imprisonment or painful death. Some were clawed with iron scrapers, others thrown into cages with leopards or bears, others roasted alive or torn limb from limb.

A Christian who died for his faith came to be known as a martyr, a Greek word meaning "witness." Martyrs bore witness to the deepest convictions of the followers of Christ. "So many suffered that the murderous ax was dulled, and the executioners grew weary," wrote Eusebius of Caesarea. Roman legions surrounded one village in Asia Minor to enforce the decree to sacrifice to the gods. When the townspeople refused, the soldiers set fire to the place, killing everyone.

In Myra, Nicholas heard the reports of the spreading horror and prepared himself. He did not have to wait long for the tromp of Roman soldiers in the street, the banging on the door, the command to surrender to Caesar's will. He followed the soldiers into the depths of a black, suffocating prison, wondering if he would ever see daylight again.

He must have asked himself that question countless times during the following years. Threats were the first weapons his captors used to break him down. When those didn't work, they tried hunger and thirst. When that failed, they moved on to beatings. Nicholas refused to renounce his beliefs. They pulled him from his cell, tortured him until he lost consciousness, then threw him back into his hole and left him alone until he grew strong enough to be tortured again.

During the long stretches when he sat and waited for the executioner's summons, Nicholas kept up his ministry. He comforted his fellow captives, urged them to keep faith, and tended the wounded as best he could. He led prayers and worship services. Occasionally he may have been able to receive visitors, and even smuggle out letters to his scattered flock. All the while, he fought to survive from one day to the next.

Meanwhile, outside the prison walls, the fires of hatred and destruction began to burn themselves out. Diocletian, weary and sick after a twenty-year reign, abdicated his throne. His successor, Galerius, redoubled the persecutions, but the people grew so sick of the bloodshed that he finally gave in. From his deathbed, Galerius issued an edict of toleration restoring rights to Christians in parts of the empire.

Then came even better news. Constantine, ruler of Rome's western provinces, led an army against another Roman leader for control of the empire. Before the battle, Constantine had a vision of a flaming *Chi-Rho* cross, a symbol of Christ, emblazoned in the sky. Beneath the cross, he saw the words, "In this sign you shall conquer." He ordered that the cross be painted on his soldier's shields, and he marched on to win the battle. In A.D. 313 Constantine issued the Edict of Milan, which granted freedom of worship to all religions, including Christianity, and ordered the return of Christian properties.

One morning the door of a dark, cold cell swung open, and a guard with a torch beckoned to the pale man sprawled on the floor inside, a man still young in age but made old in appearance by years of confinement. With faltering steps, the filthy, ragged prisoner trailed the guard down a long passageway and up damp stone stairs. At the top, a brusque voice told him he could go. Another door swung open. Nicholas, shading his eyes with trembling hands, stepped into the daylight.

CHAPTER THREE

In Service Bold as a Lion

The reign of Constantine proved to be a turning point in history. The Edict of Milan helped transform Christianity from a persecuted religion into a popular faith. Christianity spread faster than ever before. Jesus' message offered comfort in a world full of peril and suffering. His call to love God and neighbor gave meaning to hard lives.

Constantine's own enthusiasm for Christianity helped promote it through all classes of society. The emperor bestowed presents and property upon Christian congregations. He funded the construction of churches and basilicas, including St. Peter's in Rome. He declared Sunday a day of rest, placed Christian symbols on his coins, and paid for new copies of the Bible.

When Constantine decided to move his capital from Rome to the eastern part of the empire, he settled on the ancient Greek city of Byzantium. There on the banks of the Bosporus, the narrow waterway dividing Europe and Asia, he erected a glorious new city boasting palaces, gardens, public squares, and theaters. He adorned his capital with magnificent churches, testaments to the new strength of the Christian faith. Constantinople, as Byzantium was eventually renamed, became one of the world's finest cities and a center of Christianity.

Hundreds of miles away, in Myra, Nicholas shouldered the task of pulling his flock back together. There were deep wounds that needed time to heal. Mothers, fathers, and children had been lost in the Great Persecution. Livelihoods had been destroyed. Some Christians, enraged by years of oppression, took brutal revenge against their persecutors. Those who had remained steadfast in their faith often looked with deep bitterness on those who had renounced Christianity or had fled to the hills when threatened. Nicholas reminded them all of the words of Jesus: "A new commandment I give to you, that you love one another; even as I have loved you, that you also love one another" (John 13:34 RSV).

The years in prison had left Nicholas with an inward strength. Others recognized that strength, were drawn to it. People who needed hope, courage, and compassion sought him out. "All the day long he spent in labor proper to his office, listening to the requests and needs of those who came to him," we are told. "The doors of his house were open to all."

Not long after Nicholas was released from prison, famine struck Lycia. The rains stopped, rivers shrank, crops in the fields withered and died. The granaries at Myra were emptied, and people began to go hungry. As the famine spread, so did disease. The agorai filled with beggars, and every street heard the cries of those mourning the death of loved ones.

One day Nicholas got word that some grain ships en route from Alexandria to Constantinople had stopped off at Myra. He hurried down to Andriake, Myra's port, to see if the ships' captains could offer help for his starving people. By the time he got down to the harbor, an anxious crowd had gathered. He pushed his way to the front, spoke to the sailors standing guard on the wharves, and managed to arrange a conference with the captains. Nicholas wasted no time in asking for some of the grain.

"We can't do it," they answered. "The cargo was measured in Alexandria. If we arrive in Constantinople with any less, we must answer for it."

"I'm not asking you to give it away," Nicholas said. "We have good money to pay. We need grain. Come with me."

The reluctant captains followed him through the streets, where they saw for themselves the results of the famine.

"Trust in God," Nicholas told them. "Look into your hearts, and do what you know to be right."

The captains talked it over at length, and in the end they agreed to unload a portion of their grain. It was enough to help the people make it through the worst of the crisis, and it provided seed with which to plant new crops.

Many years later, a legend arose. It told how when the grain ships reached Constantinople and the captains unloaded their ships, they were dumbfounded to find that they had just as much grain in their holds as when they had left Alexandria.

ONE OF THE OLDEST stories about Nicholas depicts him as a champion of justice and protector of the innocent. According to the story, the bishop of Myra was living proof that "the righteous are bold as a lion" (Proverbs 28:1 RSV).

The Emperor Constantine, faced with a revolt in the region of Phrygia, dispatched troops under three trusted generals to quiet the unrest. Rough seas forced the troop ships to stop off at Andriake for a while. The three generals, named Ursos, Nepotianos, and Herpylion, granted their men shore leave while the ships waited to get underway again.

Before long, a brawl erupted between some of the soldiers and locals. Looting and destruction of property followed. When Nicholas heard of the trouble, he hurried down to the port.

"Where are you from, and why are you here?" he asked the three generals.

They explained that they were simply passing through.

"Well, if your mission is to promote the peace," Nicholas told them, "you're not doing a very good job, because your troops are causing trouble in my town."

The embarrassed generals quickly ordered their officers to restore order and repair any damage. Once things had quieted down, Nicholas patched things up by inviting Ursos, Nepotianos, and Herpylion to come dine with him.

As they climbed the road to Myra, they heard shouts and saw a group of citizens rushing down the hill in search of the bishop. It took Nicholas a moment to untangle the report they brought him. The local magistrate, a thoroughly corrupt man by the name of Eustathios, had accepted a bribe to sentence three innocent men to death. The victims were only moments away from execution.

Nicholas rushed to the center of town, followed by the three generals. The crowd there made way for him when they saw him coming. The three men knelt on the ground with hands bound behind their backs. The executioner stood behind them, sword raised, ready to carry out the sentence.

The bishop strode up to the executioner and grabbed the sword from his hand. He quickly untied the three bound men and set them free. The executioner made no objection.

News of what had happened raced through the streets of Myra as people streamed in and out of the town center. Hearing the excited reports, Eustathios hurried to the place of execution. When Nicholas saw him coming, he made straight for the magistrate.

"Evil man!" he cried. "You can be sure that I'll send word to Emperor Constantine about just what sort of man you are, and what sort of justice you administer."

When Eustathios saw the three generals standing at Nicholas's side, fear seized him. In a matter of seconds, the truth came out. Two city leaders, looking to get rid of some old enemies, had bribed Eustathios to condemn the men on a false charge.

At first Eustathios tried to avoid blame.

"It wasn't my doing," he insisted. "It was the wish of Eudoxius and Simonides."

"Eudoxius and Simonides are not the cause of your evil," Nicholas retorted. "It is your own greed for silver and gold."

Confronted with the facts, Eustathios confessed his sin and begged forgiveness. Nicholas demanded that the charges against the three innocent men be cleared, and he advised the magistrate to mend his ways quickly.

✳ ✳ ✳

IN THE YEAR 325, Emperor Constantine called on the bishops of the Christian Church to gather in the city of Nicaea, in northwest Asia Minor, to mend some cracks in the Church's foundation—divisions that, if left untended, might lead to a collapse. The main problem came from the teachings of a priest from Alexandria named Arius, who held that Jesus Christ was not as divine as God. Arius argued that since God created Jesus as his son, then Jesus must not have existed throughout all of time, as God had, and therefore Jesus could not be God's equal. A bitter theological dispute spread through the Church, at times even causing bloodshed.

Constantine was counting on the Christian Church to help unify his empire. A schism in the Church was a threat to his realm. The emperor decided that he would take no chances, and that he would personally preside over the Council of Nicaea.

About three hundred bishops gathered in Constantine's palace in Nicaea. The emperor, sitting on an elevated throne covered with gold leaf, opened the conference by urging unity to preserve the peace. Then the heated theological disputes began.

Tradition says that Nicholas was one of the bishops attending the great council. As he sat listening to Arius proclaim views that seemed to him blasphemous, his anger mounted. He must have asked himself: Did I suffer through all those years in prison to listen to this man betray our beliefs? His anger got the best of him. He left his seat, walked up to Arius, faced him squarely, and slapped his face.

The bishops were stunned. Arius appealed to the emperor himself.

"Should anyone who has the temerity to strike me in your presence go unpunished?" he demanded.

"Indeed, it is unlawful for anyone to lift his hand in violence before the emperor," Constantine replied. "But I will leave it to this assembly to decide whether to punish this act."

The bishops decided to strip their colleague from Myra of his clerical garments and place him under guard for the rest of the meeting. Nicholas found himself under lock and key in another wing of the palace.

But in the end, the bishop of Myra got the result he wanted. When the arguments were done, the council rebuked Arius for his beliefs. The bishops drew up a statement that came to be known as the Nicene Creed, which affirms faith in the Holy Trinity and declares that Jesus is "of one substance with the Father."

Perhaps Constantine secretly enjoyed watching someone put Arius in his place. Perhaps some of the bishops admired Nicholas for standing up forcefully, if overzealously, for his beliefs. Nicholas must have had friends and supporters in high places, because when the Council of Nicaea concluded, he was set free and his clerical robes were restored.

*　　*　　*

NICHOLAS LIVED THE REST of his years in Myra, serving his people and spreading his faith. There was so much work to be done. He spent his days praying, preaching, and laboring. Everywhere the people of Myra looked, Nicholas seemed to be there. The good bishop sat beside sickbeds, collected donations for the needy, counseled those in trouble, befriended the lonely. He baptized converts, ordained priests, married young couples, and buried the dead.

As he worked, he no doubt turned often to the words of Paul in his Letter to the Romans for a reminder of the character of true service: "Let love be genuine; hate what is evil, hold fast to what is good; love one another with brotherly affection; outdo one another in showing honor. Never flag in zeal, be aglow with the Spirit, serve the Lord" (Romans 12:9–11 RSV).

When he grew quite old, and his beard was full white,

he found that often his greatest joy came in the presence of children. He sat with them in church or in the agora, teaching them about God's love and listening to their innocent hearts. Then he knew the truth of Jesus' words: "Let the children alone, and do not hinder them from coming to Me; for the kingdom of heaven belongs to such as these" (Matthew 19:14 NASB).

Sometime around the year 340, Nicholas of Myra fell ill, and his end drew near. According to *The Golden Legend,* a late medieval account, "when it pleased our Lord to have him depart out this world, he prayed our Lord that he would send him his angels; and inclining his head he saw the angels come to him, whereby he knew well that he should depart . . . and so saying, 'Lord, into thine hands I commend my spirit,' he rendered up his soul and died." Tradition says that Nicholas died on December 6, the date now observed as his feast day.

The people of Myra, saddened by their loss, prepared a tomb of marble in the city's cathedral. They carried Nicholas's body in a torchlight procession through the town and into the church. They laid him in the crypt and said their last good-byes.

But the memories of Nicholas and his generous spirit were not done with this earth.

part two

❄

LEGENDS
OF NICHOLAS

....

CHAPTER FOUR

Nicholas the Wonderworker

t is easier to count the waves of the sea, the drops of rain, the stars, and with a glance see all the Atlantic than to recount in detail God's marvels accomplished through Saint Nicholas," an eighth-century hymn proclaimed. If one measure of a man is the stories people tell of him after he is gone, then Nicholas's life was nothing short of heroic. In the years following his death, people began to tell stories about the Bishop of Myra and his power to change people's hearts.

Looking back, they realized that his life and all the good he did was a kind of miracle. So the stories they told reflected the miraculous. They told of a man of such deep

....

faith and courage, he could accomplish things no ordinary person could.

As time went on, the storytellers embroidered the tales with their imaginations. They told of miracle after miracle. In fact, Nicholas was said to have performed so many miracles, he came to be known as the Wonderworker.

In this age of modern science, it is difficult for us to comprehend the notion of miracles. We turn with confidence to physics, chemistry, neurology, and the like to explain the extraordinary. That was not true for ancient and medieval minds. The miraculous was easier to accept in the centuries before the Scientific Revolution. In those times, the world was full of mystery and wonder. Miracles were rare but not out of place in people's comprehension of the universe.

Does that mean that we moderns must regard old legends of miracles as necessarily false? No, on two counts.

First, many old legends contain our best expressions of the human condition. They reveal the soul. Metaphors they may be, but they are metaphors that illuminate eternal truths.

Second, even in this high-tech world, it takes a pretty small mind to declare that there is absolutely no such thing as an honest-to-goodness miracle. Many of us run into a miracle or two during our lives—something that defies all rational explanation. Who is to say that God does not move in mysterious ways? As Hamlet told his friend, "There are more things in heaven and earth, Horatio, than are dreamt of in your philosophy."

ONE OF THE OLDEST stories about Nicholas tells what happened to Ursos, Nepotianos, and Herpylion, the generals who watched him save three innocent men from execution. After departing Myra, they proceeded to Phrygia, where they put down the ongoing rebellion. They returned in triumph to Constantinople, where Constantine rewarded their service.

But the three generals' success bred envy at the imperial court. Their rivals approached Ablabius, the emperor's chancellor, and began to spread lies.

"Ursos, Nepotianos, and Herpylion have conspired against the emperor," they said. "They pretend to have ended the revolt in Phrygia, but they have secretly plotted with the rebels in hopes of ruling the region themselves." To help bring Ablabius around to their way of thinking, they offered him a large bribe.

The chancellor relayed the information to Constantine. The emperor, always sensitive to reports of treachery, flew into a rage. He ordered that Ursos, Nepotianos, and Herpylion be arrested and executed the next day.

The three generals, who considered themselves to be among Constantine's most faithful commanders, were stunned when they heard of the sentence. In his despair, Nepotianos remembered how Nicholas had saved the three innocent men at Myra.

"No earthly power can save us now," he told his comrades. "Let us pray to God to protect us, as he sent Nicholas to protect the accused in Myra." They fell to their knees in prayer.

That night, the emperor dreamed that a stern, stately figure stood before him.

"Rise, emperor, and free the three men you have condemned," the vision told him. "They are unjustly accused."

"Who are you to address the emperor this way?" Constantine demanded.

"I am Nicholas, bishop of Myra, and God has sent me to tell you that these innocent men must be freed at once."

Constantine immediately sent for Ablabius. When the ashen-faced chancellor arrived, the emperor discovered that Ablabius had just had the exact same dream.

The emperor summoned the three generals.

"What magic are you using to try to free yourselves?" he demanded.

The generals didn't know what to say. Constantine realized the men were genuinely bewildered.

"Tell me," he said more kindly, "do you know a bishop named Nicholas?"

The generals suddenly took heart. They explained what they had witnessed in Myra and that they had prayed to God for the same sort of deliverance. The emperor questioned them closely and concluded that they were sincere. He freed the generals, restored them to their ranks, and loaded them down with golden treasures. The three men sailed at once for Myra and presented the gifts to Nicholas, who distributed the bags of gold among the poor.

✳   ✳   ✳

STORIES OF NICHOLAS SPREAD among crews of merchant vessels sailing in and out of Myra's port. One legend tells of a ship that ran into trouble in the eastern Mediterranean. A ferocious storm drove the vessel onto some shoals where mountainous waves threatened to break the ship to pieces. Captain and crew struggled frantically to get the ship into deeper waters, to no avail. The sailors, who had heard of Nicholas's miraculous deeds, called out to God in his name.

To their astonishment, a figure appeared out of nowhere to battle the storm by their sides. Shouting encouragement, he retied the lines holding the masts and grabbed a pole to help push the foundering ship off the shoals. Then he seized the tiller to guide the boat away from land. As soon as the ship reached safe waters, the figure vanished.

The battered vessel took refuge in Myra's port, and the mariners went straight to church to thank God for deliverance. As soon as they entered the church, they recognized the bishop standing before them as the very figure that had come to their aid in the storm. The sailors threw themselves at Nicholas's feet, but he told them to get up.

"It was not I who saved your lives," he said, "but your own faith in God."

❊   ❊   ❊

OTHER LEGENDS TELL HOW Nicholas the Wonderworker helped the poor by delivering them from hunger. It was said that one day Nicholas stopped off at a humble dwelling in the hills near the Taurus Mountains. As the family's ragged children crowded around the visitor, the embarrassed father confessed he could not invite the bishop to stay for dinner.

"We have only a little bread in the house," he said, "and it's not even enough to feed these young ones."

"Trust in the Lord," Nicholas told him. "Look in your grain bin."

The man opened the bin, which had been nearly empty the day before. He found it full to the top with grain, and the family never lacked bread for the rest of their lives.

Another story embellished Nicholas's efforts to secure grain during famine in Myra. One night the captain of a fleet of grain ships on its way to Constantinople was startled to meet a stranger on deck. The stranger, dressed as a merchant, beseeched the captain to stop off at Myra and unload some of his precious grain there. He placed three gold coins in the captain's hand before vanishing.

At first the captain thought he had imagined the whole thing, but when he opened his hand he found the three gold coins. At once he changed course for Myra, where he was astonished to recognize the merchant as Bishop Nicholas, who strode up and down the wharves directing the distribution of the ships' grain among the people.

✳ ✳ ✳

ANCIENT PAGAN DEITIES POSED a stubborn challenge for the bishop of Myra during his ministry. Worship of the Greek gods had been going on for centuries, and Nicholas realized that he must battle the old traditions for the hearts and souls of his people. He no doubt viewed pagan temples as the homes of demons and false gods, and pagan rituals as concoctions of chicanery and black magic.

His chief foe in this regard was the goddess Artemis, daughter of Zeus and sister of Apollo. Artemis was said to be the protector of seafarers, the provider of smooth seas and profitable voyages. She was also regarded as the goddess of bountiful harvests, the giver of grain. Chapter 19 of the Book of Acts tells how the Apostle Paul's teachings nearly caused a riot at Ephesus, up the coast from Myra, when the worshippers of Artemis realized that Christianity might overthrow their ancient traditions. Acts reports that "they were enraged, and cried out, 'Great is Artemis of the Ephesians!'" (Acts 19:28 RSV).

Myra boasted a temple of Artemis with grand columns surrounding an inner court and a statue of the goddess. Medieval tales of Nicholas's struggle against pagan customs depict a pitched battle with demons that lived in the temple.

"When Nicholas launched his attack against the temple," says one account, "he not only destroyed everything that towered aloft, and hurled that to earth, but he uprooted the whole from its very foundations. Indeed, what was highest, at the very pinnacle of the temple, was embedded in earth, and what was in the earth was impelled into the air." The demons, powerless to stop the assault, fled their home, shrieking.

Nicholas's war with the pagan deities continued even after his death. Legend says that a group of pilgrims were preparing to sail for Myra to visit Nicholas's tomb when an old woman approached them carrying a jar.

"Carry this jar of oil with you," she implored them. "I am too ill to make the voyage, but take this on my behalf as an offering in memory of the good bishop, and use it to fill the lamps at his shrine."

The old woman was really a demon in disguise, one of the very demons that Nicholas had forced out of the temple of Artemis. She was determined to take revenge. The jar was full of Greek fire, an explosive liquid used as a weapon in naval battles. The demon hoped to blow up Nicholas's tomb.

The unsuspecting pilgrims gladly took the jar and set sail. That night Nicholas appeared to one of them in a dream.

"Wake up, and throw that evil jar into the sea!" he warned.

At dawn, the traveler heeded the warning and pitched the jar overboard. Huge flames shot into the air so that the whole sky seemed afire. The sea began to tear apart, and the roaring waters boiled. The terrified pilgrims fell to the deck as the crew abandoned the helm. But the spirit of Nicholas guided the ship away from the burning waves, and a breeze took it safely to Myra.

THE MANY PILGRIMS VISITING Nicholas's tomb discovered yet another miracle at work: a mysterious, fragrant liquid began to seep from the bishop's remains. "And when he was buried in a tomb of marble, a fountain of oil sprang out from the head unto his feet; and unto this day holy oil issueth out of his body," reported *The Golden Legend*, the thirteenth-century collection of lore of the saints.

The sacred oil was said to have remarkable powers to heal illness. The weak, lame, blind, deaf, and dumb flocked to Myra to be cured of their ailments. The oil healed the spirit as well. When the faithful entered the church where Nicholas was buried, their worries melted away, and their hearts filled with joy.

Just one small drop of the manna of Nicholas, as the liquid came to be known, could relieve the afflicted. Pilgrims left with small vials of the manna, which they carried home to friends and loved ones. The supply of the wonderful oil seemed endless. No matter how many pilgrims arrived, the tomb rarely failed to produce the remarkable balm.

Year by year, Nicholas's fame increased. People told each other about all the good he had done while he was alive, as well as the miracles his spirit performed after death. As time passed, they began to honor the bishop with a new name: Saint Nicholas.

CHAPTER FIVE

Nicholas the Globetrotter

battered vessel with a torn lateen-rigged sail and weary crew limped into the harbor at Constantinople. Its seamen tied up to a wharf, climbed out of their ship, and threw themselves down wherever they could find a space between the heaps of cargo crowding the docks. The captain trudged onto dry land to report his arrival to the harbormaster.

"Thanks be to God! I didn't think we'd make it this time," he told a longshoreman. "I've seen weather before, but nothing like that. Saint Nicholas surely had his hand on our tiller, or we'd be at the bottom of the sea."

"Who is Saint Nicholas?"

"What? You don't know of Nicholas the Wonder-worker? Come, buy me a drink, and I'll tell you the story of how he cleared the sea lanes at Rhodes of pirates."

✳   ✳   ✳

WITH SUCH ENCOUNTERS, STORIES of Nicholas traveled the Mediterranean. Mariners in particular viewed the saint as their friend and protector. Ships leaving Myra's port carried his fame with them. Wherever they voyaged along their trade routes, sailors and merchants repeated tales of his deeds.

In ports throughout the Greek-speaking world, Christians began to dedicate chapels in memory of good Saint Nicholas. From coastal towns, his name traveled inland, up rivers linking villages in the foothills and mountains.

By the sixth century, Nicholas's reputation was established in Constantinople. The first of the city's many churches named in his honor was standing by the time of the Byzantine emperor Justinian, who reigned from 527 to 565. Constantinople, heart of the Byzantine Empire, was the great nexus of trade between East and West. From there, word of the holy saint and his marvels traveled afar.

By the seventh century, a church had been dedicated to him in Rome.

Clergymen told stories of Nicholas as examples of Christian ideals. Priests carried his name through Italy, France, and Germany. Irish monks hastened the spread in Northern Europe.

Around the year 800, a cry of terror echoed through churches and villages of Europe: "From the wrath of the Norsemen, O Lord, deliver us!" For three centuries, Vikings steered their longships into the harbors and up the rivers of Europe, conquering and pillaging as they went. The Vikings of Scandinavia—known also as Northmen or Norsemen—knew how to plunder. But they also had a genius for trade, for settling new lands, and for absorbing other cultures. They heard stories of Nicholas, and they liked what they heard. A saint who could save men from shipwreck and drowning was just right for a people who took to the seas in dragon-prow ships. The Vikings often adopted Saint Nicholas as a hero and friend.

One group of Vikings known as the Varangians, or Rus, pushed their way south on a series of rivers in an area that later came to be called "the land of the Rus," or Russia. They established trading and military posts along the banks of their rivers routes. Some settled in river towns, married into the Slavic tribes already inhabiting the countryside, and gradually came to rule the land. Kiev, on the Dnieper River, became a major center of trade and the region's capital.

In the late tenth century, a young man named Vladimir became the grand prince of Kiev. Vladimir, interested in unifying his realm with an official state religion, converted to Christianity and married Anna, sister of the Byzantine emperor, in about 988. With utmost enthusiasm, he set to work bringing Christianity to his people. He ordered noblemen and commoners alike to assemble on the banks of the Dnieper, where they waded into the river for a mass baptism.

Vladimir welcomed missionaries from Constantinople who journeyed to Kiev carrying the message of the Gospels. They also carried tales of Saint Nicholas. Stories of his miracles captured the hearts of the Russian people. The Eastern Orthodox Church flourished in Russia, and along with it the name of Saint Nicholas.

✳   ✳   ✳

FAR TO THE WEST, Viking descendents known as Normans were busy invading southern Italy. In 1071, they captured the city of Bari on Italy's southeastern coast. Soon

Bari's Norman leaders began to search for a way to bring glory to their town. They looked with envy at Venice, Bari's chief rival in trade to the north. Venice claimed Saint Mark the Evangelist as its patron. Christian pilgrims flocked there to venerate the saint's bones, which Venetian merchants had stolen from Alexandria in Egypt. In those days, the earthly remains of a saint were the most prized of all holy relics, bringing prestige and the lucrative pilgrim trade to a place lucky enough to possess them.

What we need, the merchants of Bari told themselves, is a saint who will put us in the same league as Venice.

They were in luck. From across the sea came reports of trouble in Lycia. The Byzantine Empire had lost control of much of Asia Minor to the Muslim Turks. The Lycian coast lay open to Turkish pirates who preyed on coastal towns. Myra, where the remains of Saint Nicholas lay, had fallen into Muslim hands.

There was only one thing to do—rescue the bones of the famous Saint Nicholas and bring them to Bari! When Bari merchants got wind that the Venetians were entertaining the same thoughts, they made up their minds to move fast and beat their rivals to it.

In the spring of 1087, three merchant vessels from Bari sailed into Myra's harbor. As soon as their crews had secured the ships to the wharves, two scouts disembarked to check for marauding Turks. Receiving word that the coast was clear, forty-seven armed Barians made straight for the basilica where Nicholas lay buried.

They found four monks serving in the basilica. After offering a few prayers at the altar, they politely inquired where the saint's body lay. The monks immediately grew suspicious.

"Why do you ask?" they demanded. "Are you planning to carry him away?"

The Barians hemmed and hawed for a moment, then produced their swords and declared that, yes, they had come to take Nicholas's remains to a safe place. The appalled monks tried to escape and alert the townspeople, but the Barians quickly placed them under guard.

One of the raiders, named Matthew, picked up an iron mallet and smashed his way into the white marble tomb. "Immediately such a wave of delightful perfume arose that everyone thought himself to be standing in God's paradise," reports a chronicle written shortly after the event. Matthew lowered himself into the sarcophagus, where he found the saint's remains immersed in the liquid so renowned for its healing powers. He grabbed as many bones as he could lay his hands on and handed them up to his comrades. Then the Barians made for their ships.

The monks quickly spread the alarm, and the inhabitants of Myra began hurrying down to the harbor. They gathered along the shore and begged the Barians to return the holy relics they had guarded for more than seven centuries. Some waded into the sea and tried to grab hold of the ships' rails. The Barians replied that Myra had held the honor of hosting Saint Nicholas for long enough, and that it was time for another town to have a turn. They sailed away with their booty.

After a long voyage, they reached home. The whole town turned out dockside to cheer the returning heroes. At last, Bari had a patron saint whose fame might outshine the attractions of Venice.

Almost at once, an argument broke out over whether to build a grand new basilica for Nicholas, or place his remains in the cathedral under the authority of Bari's archbishop. The dispute over who would control the priceless relics grew violent, and fighting erupted in the streets. In the end, the Barians decided to erect a basilica and tomb. Pope Urban II consecrated Saint Nicholas's new home in 1089. It would take more than a century to complete the splendid basilica, still a world-renowned example of a church built in the Romanesque style.

The miraculous healing liquid continued to flow from the relics, just as it had at Myra. The faithful streamed to Bari to worship and obtain a vial of the wondrous manna of Nicholas. The shrine became one of the most important pilgrim destinations in Christendom, almost as popular as Rome or Santiago de Compostela in Spain. For Western Europeans, Bari was a much easier place to reach than Myra, in Asia Minor. Its location on Italy's southeastern coast also made it a major port of departure and arrival for pilgrims traveling to the Holy Land. They all left Bari carrying stories of Nicholas.

In 1095, Pope Urban II called for a holy war to defend Christians in the East from Islamic rule and to capture the Holy Land from Muslim Turks. During the Crusades, Bari served as a crucial point of embarkation for Christian warriors headed to Constantinople and Jerusalem.

Knights, nobles, serfs, and adventurers from every corner of Europe gathered in the port city. The streets were filled with Crusaders bargaining for supplies, shoeing horses, readying their weapons, and stitching red crosses onto their smocks. They visited the shrine of Saint Nicholas, knelt at his tomb, and asked for his protection during difficult journeys ahead. As they traveled east through Asia Minor, they saw more churches bearing his name, and heard more tales of his wondrous deeds. When the Crusaders returned from the wars, they carried his fame back to their native lands.

BARI SOON HAD A rival center of devotion to Nicholas. Tradition says that a Crusader named Aubert from Lorraine, France, passed through Bari around the year 1098 on his way home from the Holy Land. He brought home one of Nicholas's finger bones and placed it in a chapel in a spot known as Port on the bank of the river Meurthe, in northeastern France.

The shrine became a popular destination for pilgrims, especially for merchants and boatmen traveling the river. People suffering from illness made their way to Saint-Nicolas-de-Port, as the place came to be known, in hopes of being healed. Since Nicholas had once been a prisoner, those who had escaped prison or been released from bondage also came to give thanks. They often left their chains hanging on the church's pillars as signs of gratitude.

Legend says that during the thirteenth century, a knight named Cuno de Réchicourt was captured in the Holy Land during a crusade. He remained imprisoned for four years, fastened to his cell walls by chains welded to an iron collar. Before he went to sleep on December 5, the eve of Nicholas's feast day, he prayed in the name of the saint for deliverance. His jailor mocked him, calling Nicholas a fraud, but when the knight woke, he found himself before the church of Saint-Nicolas-de-Port in France, still wearing the heavy chains.

In gratitude for his freedom, the knight gave land to the church and established an annual torchlight procession on St. Nicholas Eve. Port, once a lowly hamlet, grew into one of the wealthiest towns in Lorraine. Pilgrims rich and poor streamed to Saint-Nicolas-de-Port, including rulers such as Charles IV, the Holy Roman Emperor, and King Henry IV of England. Joan of Arc visited in 1429 to ask Nicholas to aid in her quest to drive the English out of her homeland.

The reputation of the saint traveled farther still. The Vikings dedicated a cathedral to him in Greenland. On December 6, 1492, Christopher Columbus dropped anchor off the northwestern coast of what is now Haiti and gave the name St. Nicholas Mole to a port he found there. He also bestowed Nicholas's name on a nearby cape and on a channel off the northwestern coast of Cuba. Spaniards following in his wake named a settlement St. Nicholas Ferry in the area that is now Jacksonville, Florida.

Saint Nicholas had reached the New World.

CHAPTER SIX

Nicholas the International Phenomenon

$\mathcal{I}$f in the Indies some man is afflicted, or if there be in the British Isles some victim of calumny, if he but invoke the name of Nicholas, then Nicholas will arrive to succor him," enthused one of the saint's admirers during the ninth century. By that time, Nicholas was well on his way to becoming the medieval equivalent of an international celebrity. From Paris to Rome to Constantinople, Christians called upon him as a champion of justice and a benefactor to those in need—a true "people's victor." By some accounts, he was the most popular saint after Mary, mother of Jesus.

By the end of the fifteenth century, more than 2,500

churches, chapels, monasteries, hospitals, schools, and works of art had been dedicated to Nicholas in Western Europe. England alone boasted nearly 400 Nicholas churches. The stained-glass windows of cathedrals such as those at Tours and Chartres in France told glowing stories of the saint's deeds. Paintings, mosaics, carvings, and statues depicted him with a crown of white hair and a white beard, dressed in a bishop's vestments, his right hand raised to bless.

Priests wrote accounts of Nicholas's life and the miracles attributed to him. Based on oral traditions, such "lives of the saints" were not what we would call biographies so much as collections of stories representing Christian ideals. The earliest surviving Life of Nicholas, dating from the eighth or ninth century, was set down in Constantinople by a scribe known as Michael the Archimandrite. Many others followed. Clergymen often read from a Life of Nicholas to congregations on his feast day, December 6.

Prayers, hymns, and liturgical services inspired by Nicholas appeared. A traditional Catholic prayer invokes his name in asking for the protection of the innocent.

God, Who didst grace the Blessed Nicholas as protector of imperiled innocence whilst he lived, and after his death by countless miracles, grant that by his merits we

*may be freed from perversion of justice while alive and
from the fires of Gehenna (hell) after death.*

AROUND THE TWELFTH CENTURY, Saint Nicholas became a star of the stage. Miracle plays, an early form of modern drama, reenacted stories about the saints. Playwrights cast Nicholas in the leading role of some of the first productions. They were often raucous affairs, filled with humor and mock violence. Audiences gathered before outdoor stages in town squares to cheer as Nicholas battled thieves, chased down murderers, and tricked con artists in defense of those who called on him.

Children were often named after saints, so the Greek name *Nikólaos* made its way from language to language: in English, Nicholas, Nick, Collin; in French, Nicole, Collette, Colienne; in Italian, Niccolò, Nicola, Cola; in German, Klaus, Niklas, Nico; in Spanish, Nicolás, Coleta; in Dutch, Niklass, Klaas; in Russian, Nikolai, Kolya. Those are just a few of the variations. Emperors, princes, tsars, and popes shared the saint's name.

Cities, regions, and even countries revered Saint Nicholas so much that they chose him as a patron saint: Greece; the Netherlands; Norway; Sicily; Apulia, Italy; Lorraine, France; Fribourg, Switzerland; Aberdeen, Scotland; Limerick, Ireland; and Portsmouth, England, just to name a few. In Belgium, a town was named Sint-Niklaas.

In no place was Nicholas more loved than in Russia. Peasants counted on Nikolai Ugodnik, Nicholas the Helper, to watch after the crops, preserve homes from fires, and help shepherds guard their flocks. On St. Nicholas Day, it was said, no wolf would harm even a chicken. "If anything happens to God, we've always got St. Nicholas," went an old Russian proverb. Thursday prayers were dedicated to the saint, and Russian children learned to offer their prayers to God "through Jesus Christ and Saint Nicholas."

One Sunday, goes an old Russian tale, a husband and wife were walking home from church in Kiev with their baby. As they crossed the Dnieper, the infant slipped from the mother's arms and went over the side of the bridge, into the swift-flowing water. The desperate parents ran up and down the river bank to no avail, then fell on their knees and prayed in the name of Saint Nicholas for a miracle that would save their loved one.

The next morning, when the sacristan went to open the doors of the cathedral, he was startled to hear a baby's cry. Beneath the icon of Saint Nicholas he found the child, still soaking wet but unharmed. Such were the deeds of Nikolai Chudotvorets, Nicholas the Wonder-worker, in Russia.

SO BELOVED, SO ADMIRED was Saint Nicholas, it seemed that everyone wanted to claim him. "The clerk and the soldier, the tiller of the soil, women, the sailor, the merchant pay thanks to Nicholas," explained Alexander of Villedieu, a French scholar, at the outset of the thirteenth century. Bankers, butchers, millers, grocers, brewers, tanners, candle makers, firefighters, and apothecaries all looked to him as their special patron. So did travelers, school children, orphans, students, poets, unmarried girls, spinsters, lovers, newlyweds, peasants—the list goes on and on. He became a sort of every-saint, one for all people and all causes.

Stories of Nicholas calming waves and rescuing seamen inspired mariners to consider him their patron. When a ship was put to sea, it was not uncommon to hear sailors wish each other good luck with the cry, "May Saint Nicholas hold the tiller!" In some places, when leaving port the sailors would throw three loaves of bread onto the water, known as "Saint Nicholas loaves," to help ensure smooth sailing.

Seamen bestowed Nicholas's name on countless harbors, capes, islands, channels, and shoals around the world. Chapels dedicated to him dotted coastlines. Sailors returning safely to port lit votive candles beside icons of Nicholas. They left shells painted with his image or little carved ships as tokens of affection.

An old Serbian legend tells of Nicholas's devotion to mariners. One day all the saints had gathered to enjoy a cup of wine, which they passed around their circle. When it reached Nicholas, who was showing signs of sleepiness, the cup slipped from his fingers and fell onto the floor. Saint Elias shook his arm to wake him up.

"Please excuse my clumsiness," Nicholas told the others. "I've been quite absent from your company just now. The sea is stormy tonight, and I had to help three hundred ships in danger of sinking. It has made me tired and caused me to lose my grip."

His patronage naturally spread to trades associated with the sea or water. Fishermen, bargemen, dock workers, ferrymen, chandlers (suppliers of ships), navigators, ships' carpenters, victims of shipwrecks, and bridge tenders all looked to Nicholas. Pumpers and firefighters regarded him as their friend.

Because merchants were often seamen or depended on

seagoing trade routes, they took Nicholas as their patron. In harbor towns that bustled with commerce, his name was well known. He became a favorite of merchants who traded by land as well. One old story tells of a trader returning from the Orient with a caravan loaded with silk, spices, ivory, and jade. As he made his way along a narrow trail in a treacherous mountain pass, a storm blew up the valley with lashing winds and driving snow. The camels behind him panicked and plunged off the trail into the chasm below.

The trader, realizing he would be lucky to make it out of the pass alive, prayed in Saint Nicholas's name. The storm subsided, and the ruined man trudged sorrowfully down the mountain. Several miles further, he rounded a bend and stopped in his tracks, unable to believe his eyes. There stood his entire caravan—camels, riders, goods, and all—safe and sound, waiting for him.

Prosperous merchants often lent money, so Nicholas's patronage soon extended to bankers, who looked to him as a protector of bargains made in good faith. Pawnbrokers adopted the saint as well. Their symbol, three golden balls, symbolized the three bags of gold that Nicholas tossed through a window in Patara to save the poor man's three daughters. To this day, signs bearing three balls hang at the doors of pawn shops.

Grain dealers, recalling stories of how the saint found grain for Myra, chose Nicholas as their patron. So did artisans in the cloth business, perhaps because of influential churches dedicated to the saint in Flanders and Lorraine, regions where their trade flourished. Weavers, drapers, lace makers, button makers, shear men, linen merchants, and cloth merchants invoked his name.

The reputation of the fragrant healing oil that flowed from Nicholas's relics brought pharmacists, perfumers, florists, and bottlers into his circle. Since Nicholas was known as the "people's victor" and champion of justice, he became the patron of lawyers, judges, and clerks of court. Even thieves and highwaymen claimed him. After all, in those days of rough justice, their trickery was not too far removed from merchants' haggling and horse trading.

Maidens of marriageable age, remembering how Nicholas provided dowries with his three bags of gold, regarded him as their helper. The same story made him the patron of newlyweds and happy marriages. Since Nicholas's mother, Nonna, had prayed so long and hard for a child, he became the patron saint of couples who hoped to have children.

DURING THE LATE MIDDLE AGES, Nicholas gained a new sort of fame. Especially in Western Europe, people came to view him as the patron saint of children. Numerous legends told how he snatched babies, children, and students from the jaws of disaster. Two old stories, one from the West and one from the East, are examples of his love for young people everywhere.

The first legend, though strange and gory, became one of the most famous Nicholas tales in Western Europe. It was often performed in miracle plays in town squares or in front of churches.

One day three young theology students traveling to a monastery school stopped for the night at a country inn. The keen-eyed innkeeper noticed that their purses were heavy, and he and his wife laid plans to steal all their money. That night, while the students slept, he crept into their room and killed them. To hide his awful deed, he cut up their bodies and stuffed them into casks used for salting meat.

The next day Saint Nicholas arrived at the tavern disguised as a beggar and asked for a bite to eat.

"We have nothing to serve you," the innkeeper told him. "The larder is empty."

"You lie!" Nicholas roared, and he forced his way into the back room, where he discovered the gruesome evidence. At once he fell to his knees in prayer. As the inn-keeper and his wife cowered, the miraculous came to pass: the three innocent students came back to life.

The tale was told and retold in scores of ways. With time, the victims became three children who fell into the hands of an evil butcher who put them in a pickle barrel. The image of three youngsters rising out of a barrel is still one of the most widely known symbols of Saint Nicholas in paintings and stained-glass art.

✳   ✳   ✳

THE SECOND LEGEND, FROM THE EAST, is a kid-napping tale. Many years after Nicholas's death, the people of Myra were celebrating the good saint on the eve of his feast day. Without warning, while the ceremonies were taking place, Arab pirates from Crete swarmed ashore and ransacked the town. On the way back to their ships, they grabbed a boy named Basileos and carried him away as a slave.

The emir of Crete chose Basileos to be one of his household servants. The boy became his cupbearer, and he stood behind his master at every meal, waiting to refill his jeweled cup with wine.

The months passed slowly for the homesick boy. A year to the day after he had been kidnapped, he stood at the emir's table looking downcast.

"What makes you so sad today?" the emir asked him.

"I am thinking of my home and the feast of Saint Nicholas there," he replied softly.

"You will never see Myra again!" his master told him.

Suddenly Basileos heard a clap of thunder and saw the emir's court dissolving before his eyes. Just as he felt his feet go out from under him, he had a vision of Saint Nicholas offering his blessing.

Meanwhile, back in Myra, Basileos's family was observing the painful anniversary of the loss of their son. As they sat down to eat, their dogs began barking in the courtyard. The father opened the door, and there stood a dazed Basileos, dressed in Cretan garb, still holding the emir's jeweled cup.

Such legends made Nicholas the benefactor of children everywhere. As the centuries passed, and the Middle Ages gave way to ages of science and reason, his patronage for other groups slowly faded. But his role as the champion of children would endure.

part three

❄

LEGACY OF
NICHOLAS

....

CHAPTER SEVEN

A Bringer of Gifts

wilight falls on a remote village somewhere in northern France, about seven or eight centuries ago. It is December 5, the eve of Saint Nicholas Day. Anticipation is mounting, especially among the children. Moments ago, the little town center was crowded with spectators who gathered to watch the day's hero battle villains and demons in a play staged on the church steps. The play is done, and the villagers drift away, the youngsters tugging their parents' hands to hurry them along.

As soon as they get home, the children place their shoes carefully beside their bed or the fireplace. Then they dive under the covers, visions of treats dancing in their heads.

....

Every boy and girl knows that later that night, when all are asleep, Saint Nicholas will pass through town.

When they wake the next morning, if they've been good, they'll find their shoes filled with all sorts of delights: fruit, nuts, sugar candy, maybe a coin or two. Those who've been unruly or failed to learn their catechism might find a small stick among the goodies, a miniature switch representing a rebuke for naughtiness.

Later that day, mothers will hand out cakes to eat beside the blazing hearth. The village boys will troop from door to door, singing in return for sweets. Neighbors will visit to exchange good cheer. Everyone will gather at church for hymns and prayers in remembrance of the beloved saint.

IN THIS SCENE FROM the late Middle Ages, we find Saint Nicholas at work in the role we associate with him today. That role as a bringer of gifts doubtless grew out of the old stories about him, especially the story of his night visits to the home with three maidens where he left three bags of gold. Across Europe, people associated his name with generosity. The theologian Thomas Aquinas, in his thirteenth-century *Summa Theologica*, extolled Nicholas's gift-giving as an example of kindness made all the greater because it was offered in secret. The poet Dante, in his fourteenth-century *Purgatorio*, evoked "the liberality of Nicholas to the maidens" as a model of giving.

At some point during the Middle Ages, people began exchanging presents on Saint Nicholas Day. The custom of distributing gifts to the young may have begun in schools, where schoolmasters made December 6 a holiday since Nicholas was the patron saint of scholars. Teachers often gave the students small gifts as rewards for their work. The students, in return, offered tokens of appreciation.

According to some, the tradition of gifts appearing overnight began with nuns in France who left nuts, cakes, and even oranges from Spain on the doorsteps of poor families on the eve of Saint Nicholas Day. Or it may have begun with parents who saw miracle plays about the saint's generosity and decided to imitate it for their own children.

In some places, children filled their shoes with straw and carrots for the white horse that Nicholas was said to ride on his midnight journey. The saint came into the house through a window, even if it was shut—a trick he had learned, no doubt, during his days of delivering gold through a window in Patara. In some homes, Saint Nicholas appeared in person before children went to bed on the eve of his feast day. The kindly old gentleman, decked in his vestments, quizzed them on their studies and inquired if they had been good. Youngsters in northern Germany notched a stick every time they said their prayers so they could show Nicholas the evidence of their piety.

Since Nicholas had been so young when elected bishop of Myra, cathedrals in various European towns celebrated December 6 by selecting a youngster to assume an honored place. The boy bishop, robed in vestments and wearing a miter, blessed the people, delivered sermons, collected alms, and led visitations to nearby churches. He appointed his friends as priests and cannons, while the real priests and cannons assumed the role of choirboys. The boy bishop's reign lasted until December 28, the Feast of the Holy Innocents.

The custom was meant partly to instill reverence in young people. The boy bishop and his helpers were expected to learn about the important rituals of the church. But the season was also full of the kind of pranks and revelry you might expect when children are put in charge. The boy bishop could declare holidays and hand out goodies. Sometimes he became the Lord of Misrule, who pre-

sided over rowdy parties, dances, and torchlight parades
fueled by a good deal of wine and beer. As the years
passed, the celebrations grew so raucous that people began
to complain. England's King Henry VIII tried to put an
end to the "unfitting and inconvenient usages," which he
viewed as "rather to the derision than any true glory of
God."

IN 1517, MARTIN LUTHER nailed his Ninety-five
Theses to a church door in Wittenberg, Germany, setting
off an upheaval that eventually split Christendom in two.
Luther accused religious officials of being more concerned
with money and power than with saving souls, and chal-
lenged the Church to reform itself. Christianity divided
into Catholics and Protestants. The latter took aim at what
they viewed as problems in the Catholic Church, from
elaborate rituals to the sale of high offices.

As they founded new churches, Protestant reformers
turned their fire on traditions surrounding the saints. They
scoffed at the idea of calling on divine superheroes for aid.
Luther called the invocation of saints "a fond [foolish]
thing, vainly invented." Stories of miracles conjured by

saints were mere superstitions. Holy relics were pig bones, and cure-all holy balms mere snake oil. The custom of giving alms or buying candles when asking favors of saints was nothing but popish trickery, a racket to extort money from desperate people and guilty consciences. Pilgrimages were a waste of money better spent on the poor.

Reformers decried gilded images of saints, which they viewed as false idols. They pulled sculptures from church niches and ripped paintings from frames. The most zealous launched a wholesale destruction of priceless artwork. Stained-glass windows depicting saints' deeds were smashed. Stone statues were knocked to pieces and wooden ones burned. Scenes painted on walls were whitewashed. Pages containing lives of the saints were used to polish boots or wrap up fish.

Dozens of saints' days filled the calendar, holidays when work came to a stop. Protestants and their burgher allies regarded them as opportunities for idleness, drunkenness, and vagabondage. In England, Puritans put an end to the feast days, among other rituals.

Advances in science did not help the saints' reputations. The telescope and the microscope pierced the veil of the natural world, and much mystery drained out of the old miracle stories. An age of inquiry replaced an age of faith. As the scholar Charles W. Jones observed, "Holy wells became mineral baths."

Nicholas was by no means immune to this assault. Miracle plays performed around December 6 began to disappear. The hymns and prayers celebrating Nicholas's deeds fell out of use. Reformers tried to discourage the lighting of candles, exchanging of gifts, and distribution of sweets to children on Saint Nicholas Day.

By the end of the sixteenth century, Nicholas had been banished from religious life in much of Western Europe. But he could not be driven out of people's hearts and imaginations. He was much too beloved for that to happen. When Saint Nicholas lost his honored place in churches, something extraordinary happened. He moved into homes, where he had legions of fans, especially among children. He became a hero of the hearth. As a folk hero, he took on a new guise—or, rather, several new guises.

✳   ✳   ✳

SEVERAL HUNDRED YEARS AGO, Spanish kings controlled the Netherlands. The Spanish court sent governors to look after Dutch ports and bishops to look after Dutch souls. From time to time, a Spanish bishop would appear in Holland and make himself known by distributing gifts to children and the needy. That is why Dutch children can tell you with assuredness all about Sinterklaas, as they call Saint Nicholas. Sinterklaas lives in Spain and visits the Netherlands once a year dressed in a bishop's red finery.

During much of the Middle Ages, southern Spain was ruled by Arabic-speaking Muslims from North Africa known as Moors. The Spaniards eventually defeated the Moors, so it seemed only natural that Sinterklaas should have at his side a Moorish servant named Zwarte Piet, or Black Peter. According to Dutch lore, Sinterklaas spends most of the year in Spain, keeping track of who's been good and who's been bad in a big red ledger. Every November, with Black Peter's help, he packs up his presents for all the children who have made his good list and sets sail for the Netherlands.

Upon his arrival, the white-bearded saint travels from town to town, checking up on children to see if they are behaving. At night, he flies over rooftops on a great white horse, listening at the chimneys to confirm his suspicions. Before going to bed on Saint Nicholas's Eve, Dutch children set out their shoes in hopes of gifts. Black Peter has the job of slipping down chimneys to leave presents and collect any carrots, straw, and sugar left for Nicholas's white horse. He might leave a switch as a warning for naughty children. If they've been horribly bad, he might even carry them off in a sack.

In much of France, Père Noël (Father Christmas) replaced Saint Nicholas as the bringer of gifts. Père Noël wears a white beard and a long, hooded red robe trimmed in white fur. Often he travels with a donkey, who carries his basket of toys and treats. His helper, Père Fouettard (Father Whipper) sometimes follows behind, recognizable by his mangy gray beard, dirty dark robe, and whip. Père Fouttard, like Black Peter, deals with disobedient children.

Italy's gift bringer is Befana, a genial hook-nosed old woman who wears patched clothes and carries a broom. One day, as Befana was sweeping her floor, she heard a knock at her door. She opened it to find three finely dressed men who asked the way to Bethlehem. They invited her to come with them to worship the Christ Child, who had just been born, but she declined, saying that she had too many chores to do. After they left she changed her mind and hurried after them, broom in hand. But she never caught up with the three Magi. To this day she seeks the Christ Child, checking each house where children live and leaving gifts behind.

Northern Germany saw the appearance of the Weih-
nachtsmann (Christmas Man), an old man who trudged
through the snow carrying a small Christmas tree over his
shoulder. In other parts of Germany, Switzerland, and
Austria, the Christkindel (Christ Child) became the present bringer. Protestant reformers, who wanted to teach
children that gifts come directly from God, painted the
Christkindel as a little angel with golden wings and flaxen
hair. German immigrants later carried the Christkindel tradition to the United States, changing the name to Kriss
Kringle. (The Christkindel faded in America, and Kriss
Kringle became another name for Santa Claus.)

In England, Father Christmas pushed Saint Nicholas
aside as the master of ceremonies for December celebrations. Father Christmas did not bring gifts, but he repre-
sented the mirth and generosity of the season. He was
often pictured as a hearty, holly-crowned fellow clothed in
green or scarlet robes who brought food, wine, and revelry
to every Christmas feast. In *A Christmas Carol*, Charles
Dickens turned Father Christmas into his Ghost of Christmas Present.

Ancient Scandinavian lore told of the Little People,
mischievous gnomes who inhabited the countryside and
sometimes played tricks on humans. When in a bad mood,

the Little People might ruin crops, curdle milk, or even start fires. If in good humor, they secretly helped with the chores and looked after the farm.

Over time, the Little People came to be associated with the Christmas season in Scandinavia. Every household was said to have at least one Christmas elf, called the Jultomte in Sweden and Julenisse in other parts of Scandinavia. (*Jul* means Yule, or Christmastime. *Nisse*, perhaps by coincidence, is an old variation of the name Nicholas.) The elves spend most of the year sleeping under stairways and other dark out-of-the-way places. But at Christmastime they creep out of hiding, dressed in little red pointed caps, and make themselves known in sly ways. Children leave out plates of cookies or saucers of milk to keep them in good humor. If the elves are pleased, they spread good cheer and leave behind presents for young ones to find.

Thus in Western Europe, Nicholas slowly blended into various folk traditions associated with December celebrations. In Eastern Europe, Asia Minor, and the vast Russian empire, where Orthodox Church traditions prevailed, Nicholas held onto his place as a revered saint. But people in the East regarded him more as the Wonderworker than as a gift bringer.

Then came the opening of the New World. Immigrants streamed to America, many carrying centuries-old memories of Saint Nicholas and Nicholas-like figures. In the United States, the good old saint was destined to transform himself once again.

....

CHAPTER EIGHT

A Long and Circuitous Route

he road and seaway from Myra in Asia Minor to your street corner and chimney at Christmas is a long one, and was long in the building," reported the venerable *American Heritage* magazine a half century ago. "Nevertheless, it is there, and one traveler voyages the incredibly long and circuitous route each year. He is somewhat metamorphosed, to be sure, as a result of the journey, but he is still one and the same: St. Nicholas and Santa Claus."

The last leg of that long and circuitous route crosses the landscape of United States history. It's as American as any story can be.

....

In 1624, a group of families sponsored by the Dutch West India Company arrived at the mouth of the Hudson River to launch a colony they called New Netherland. The colonists set up a trading post on Manhattan Island, which they famously bought from the Indians for twenty-four dollars' worth of trade goods. The post quickly turned into a busy port called New Amsterdam.

The early Dutch settlers no doubt brought with them memories of Sinterklaas, as they called Saint Nicholas, and his habit of leaving goodies in empty shoes on the eve of his feast day back in Holland. Some of them may have kept up the old tradition for a while in their New World home. But most of the New Amsterdam colonists belonged to the Dutch Reformed Church. Like the Puritans in New England, they were not keen on holidays celebrating saints. Whatever Saint Nicholas customs they imported did not take strong root.

In 1664, four English warships sailed into New Amsterdam's harbor, aimed their cannons at the homes of the Dutch merchants, and demanded that they surrender the island. The outgunned Dutch handed over the settlement, which the English renamed New York, in honor of the Duke of York, brother of King Charles II. Dutch colonists stayed in New York as influential citizens. Under British rule, memories of Sinterklaas faded even more.

✳   ✳   ✳

NOW FAST FORWARD TO the early nineteenth century, a time when New Yorkers, like other Americans, were full of pride for their infant republic. John Pintard, a businessman and prominent citizen of New York City, had Saint Nicholas on his mind.

Pintard was a brilliant promoter. "He could indite a handbill that would inflame the minds of the people for any good work," wrote a biographer. "He could call a meeting with the pen of a poet, and before the people met, he would have arranged the doings for a perfect success." Pintard played a role in launching New York City's first fire insurance company, its first savings bank, and its free school system. He had a hand in starting the American Bible Society and the General Theological Seminary of the Episcopal Church, and promoted the digging of the Erie Canal.

John Pintard was also an ardent patriot and lover of history. He helped establish Washington's Birthday and the Fourth of July as national holidays. In 1804, he had a leading part in founding the New-York Historical Society.

"Old customs" and "ancient usages" were of keen interest to Pintard. As he studied his city's past, its Dutch roots caught his fancy. He believed all good New Yorkers should know something of that history as a matter of civic pride. Pintard was aware of the old Dutch tradition of annual visits by a gift-bearing Sinterklaas. Saint Nicholas, he decided, could serve as a good reminder of New York's proud heritage.

In fact, Pintard reasoned, the old fellow would make a good patron saint for both the New-York Historical Society and the city of New York. During the society's annual banquet in January 1809, one of its members offered this toast: "To the memory of Saint Nicholas. May the virtuous habits and simple manners of our Dutch ancestors not be lost in the luxuries and refinements of the present time."

At that same banquet, Pintard and his friends welcomed a new member to the New-York Historical Society, a young writer named Washington Irving. Best remembered today for his stories "The Legend of Sleepy Hollow" and "Rip Van Winkle," Irving had made up his mind to write a tongue-in-cheek history of New York's early days. His *History of New-York from the Beginning of the World to the End of the Dutch Dynasty* was published on Saint Nicholas Day, December 6, 1809.

Irving wrote his mock history under the pseudonym Diedrich Knickerbocker. The surname *Knickerbocker* was a popular term for New Yorkers of Dutch ancestry. It literally means "toy marble-baker" and refers to an old Dutch custom of making children's marbles from baked dough balls.

Diedrich Knickerbocker happily informed his readers that the first Dutch colonists had sailed to New Amsterdam in a ship that boasted a "a goodly image of St. Nicholas" carved on its bow, a figure "equipped with a low, broad-brimmed hat, a huge pair of Flemish trunk-hose, and a pipe that reached to the end of the bowsprit." Soon after the settlers had disembarked, Saint Nicholas appeared to one of them in a dream to show them where they should build their new city.

"And lo, the good St. Nicholas came riding over the tops of the trees," Irving wrote, "in that self-same waggon wherein he brings his yearly presents to children. . . . And he lit his pipe by the fire, and sat himself down and smoked; and as he smoked the smoke from his pipe ascended into the air, and spread like a cloud over head." After indicating the best spot for building, he put his pipe in his hat band, and "laying his finger beside his nose," he mounted his wagon and disappeared over the treetops.

Irving referred to Nicholas about two dozen times in his imaginary history. He wrote that "the good St. Nicholas would often make his appearance in his beloved city, of a holiday afternoon, riding jollily among the tree tops, or over the roofs of the houses, now and then drawing forth magnificent presents from his breeches pockets, and dropping them down the chimneys of his favourites." Readers loved the whimsical story and its flying Dutch-American Saint Nick.

Meanwhile, the busy John Pintard continued his efforts. On December 6, 1810, at a New-York Historical Society dinner, he distributed a pamphlet featuring Saint Nicholas dressed as a bishop. Nearby, stockings hung by a fireplace, one stuffed with presents for a good little girl, the other laden with switches for a bad boy. The pamphlet's verse read, in part:

SAINT NICHOLAS, my dear good friend!
To serve you ever was my end,
If you will, now, me something give,
I'll serve you ever while I live.

WE COME NOW TO Clement Clarke Moore and his poem, which by some estimates has been reprinted more times than any other American verse.

Moore was a wealthy and learned man, a scholar of Hebrew, a professor of biblical languages at the General Theological Seminary in New York. He lived with his family in a big imposing house on a ninety-four-acre Manhattan estate known as Chelsea, which stretched from what is now Nineteenth Street to Twenty-fourth Street, and from Eighth Avenue to Tenth Avenue. (To this day, this area of New York City is known as Chelsea.)

According to tradition, in 1822, on the afternoon of Christmas Eve, Moore climbed into a horse-drawn sleigh and set off to buy a turkey for his family's Christmas feast. As he rode to market, sleigh bells jingling and whip cracking in the cold air, a poem began to take shape in his mind.

He wrote it down as soon as he returned home, and that evening he sat by the fireside, gathered his children around him, and read aloud for the first time "A Visit from St. Nicholas." His children adored the story-poem of the right jolly old elf with the little round belly that shook when he laughed, like a bowl full of jelly. So did a visiting family friend, who made a copy and took it home with her. The verse made its way to the *Troy Sentinel* in upstate New York, which published it a year later, on December 23, 1823.

The editor of the *Sentinel*, in his introductory note, admitted that "We know not to whom we are indebted for the following description of that unwearied patron of children." For many years, newspapers and magazines reprinted "A Visit from Saint Nicholas" as an anonymous work. It is said that Clement Moore, learned professor that he was, did not want to be identified as the author of such a trifle. He did not publish it under his own name until 1844. By that time, it had become a national favorite.*

With Moore's poem, the American Saint Nicholas was born. He wore not a bishop's robes or a Dutch burgher's jacket but "was dressed all in fur, from his head to his foot." It was a perfect choice of wardrobe for a time when men like John Jacob Astor had made fortunes in the American fur trade.

Moore had plenty of material to draw on when composing his verse. As a seminary professor, he was familiar with Saint Nicholas's ancient reputation. He had probably seen his friend John Pintard's pamphlet with its image

....

* Some scholars have argued that a writer named Henry Livingston was the true author of "A Visit from Saint Nicholas," not Clement C. Moore. No one knows for sure. For the sake of tradition, if nothing else, I will stick with Moore. To paraphrase Charles Dickens, the wisdom of our ancestors is in the account of Moore's authorship, and my unhallowed hands shall not disturb it, or the country's done for.

....

of stockings hung by the chimney (a tradition reportedly begun in Italy and France, where convent girls hung up their stockings on Saint Nicholas Eve in hopes of finding them filled with little gifts the next morning). He had read Washington Irving's *History of New York* with its description of Saint Nicholas "laying his finger beside his nose."

The gnomes of Scandinavia who bring presents at Christmastime may have supplied Moore with the idea of turning his Saint Nicholas into a right jolly old elf. And some folklorists suggest that his coursers came from the frozen climes of Siberia and Lapland, where people told stories of magic men who rode the night sky with the aid of flying reindeer. It seems more likely that Moore got the idea of flying reindeer from an 1821 book called *The Children's Friend*, which included this verse:

Old Santeclaus with much delight
His reindeer drives this frosty night.
O'er chimney tops, and tracks of snow,
To bring his yearly gifts to you.

"'Twas the Night Before Christmas," as Clement Moore's poem came to be known, depicted Saint Nicholas's visit not on the eve of December 6, Saint Nicholas Day, but on December 24. Thus Christmastime became Saint Nick time in the United States.

The poem had one other remarkable effect. For centuries, Christmas had included a rowdy side, one with much drinking, noisemaking, and gangs of boisterous youth wandering the streets demanding hospitality from neighbors. The party season dated to pre-Christian times, when ancient cultures celebrated the winter solstice with merrymaking. The festivities often got out of hand, which was one reason that Puritans and other reformers took a dim view of Christmas celebrations. Moore's poem, with its images of the quiet hearth and children nestled all snug in their beds, helped make Christmas a home-centered, family-oriented time. Christmas became a holiday for children.

By the time of Moore's poem, Saint Nicholas was assuming a new name in the United States. Americans found foreign terms for Saint Nicholas—particularly the Dutch Sinterklaas and German Sankt Niklaus—difficult to pronounce. As they often did with old European words, they simply Americanized the name to Santa Claus.

FROM THE 1820S UNTIL the Civil War, artists depicted Santa Claus in all sorts of outfits. Sometimes he wore a Dutch three-cornered hat, sometimes knickerbockers, sometimes a cape. It fell to Thomas Nast, the German-born political cartoonist who gave us the Republican elephant and Democratic donkey, to help Americans settle on a visual image of Santa.

In an 1863 illustration for *Harper's Weekly*, Nast showed Santa Claus dressed in a stars-and-stripe suit distributing gifts to Union troops. During the next three decades, he produced numerous woodcut images of Santa coming down chimneys, filling stockings, and watching over sleeping children. With time, Nast's Santa Claus became a rotund, jolly old elf dressed in a red fur-trimmed jacket with a broad belt, boots, and a cap—a Santa that fit the spirit of Clement Moore's poem.

During the period Nast was at work, Americans were fascinated with the idea of reaching the North Pole. The public devoured news reports of expeditions into the mysterious icy latitudes. Nast decided the North Pole would be a good home for Santa, who could spy on children around the world with a long telescope. His pen produced drawings of Santa's workshop full of toys, Santa's list of good and bad children, and Santa's stacks of letters from youngsters all over the globe.

The Industrial Revolution brought factory-made toys, and Santa's magic bag overflowed with gifts. Parents across the country became secret Santas, often with a little help from the Sears catalog. "We shall have an old-fashioned Christmas tree for the grandchildren upstairs, and I shall be their Santa Claus myself," President Benjamin Harrison said of his White House holiday plans in 1891. "If my influence goes for aught in this busy world, I hope that my example will be followed by every family in the land."

By the early 1900s, Santa had claimed the leading role in America's commercial Christmas pageant. He appeared on Christmas cards, in newspaper advertisements, in department stores, in stories and plays, even in the new moving pictures. Norman Rockwell put him on the cover of the *Saturday Evening Post*.

In 1924, Macy's department store in New York City held its first Thanksgiving Day Parade welcoming Santa Claus to Herald Square. About that time, the post office in Santa Claus, Indiana, began receiving thousands of letters each year addressed to Santa Claus. Tourist attractions such as Santa's Candy Castle and Santa Claus Land later sprang up. The year 1937 saw the opening of the first training school for department store Santas, in Albion, New York.

Clement Moore had described Santa Claus as a "little old driver" in a "miniature sleigh." Thomas Nast had followed his lead with plump gnome-sized figures. In the first half of the twentieth century, Santa's physique expanded in every direction, especially with the brushwork of Swedish-American artist Haddon Sundblom.

In 1931, the Coca-Cola Company commissioned Sundblom to paint Santa Claus for an advertisement campaign. For the next thirty-five years, Sundblom created Coca-Cola ads that showed a big, hearty Santa holding children in his lap, playing with electric trains, raiding the refrigerator, and, of course, drinking Coke. People saw the ads everywhere, in magazines, on billboards, in drugstore soda fountains. The image of the warm, smiling, robust Santa Claus that most Americans have today came largely from those ads.

One more important addition came in a 1939 promotional giveaway from Chicago's Montgomery Ward department store. Advertising editor Robert Lewis May came up with the idea of an illustrated booklet with a story about a red-nosed reindeer named Rudolph, who guides Santa's sleigh. Montgomery Ward gave out millions of the booklets. In 1947, songwriter Johnny Marks composed a song based on May's story. Gene Autry, "the Singing Cowboy," recorded the song two years later, spreading Rudolph's fame around the globe.

By the mid-twentieth century, the long and circuitous route was complete. Saint Nicholas the bishop, never strong in the American tradition to begin with, had almost completely disappeared in the United States. In his place, Santa Claus had come to town.

....

CHAPTER NINE

A Legacy Full of God's Love

$\mathcal{I}$ have been extra good this year, so I have a long list of presents I want," young Sally writes to Santa Claus in the TV classic *A Charlie Brown Christmas*. "Please note the size and color of each item, and send as many as possible. If it seems too complicated, make it easy on yourself. Just send money. How about tens and twenties?"

Every December, millions tune in to watch Charlie Brown struggle to find the true meaning of Christmas. The program is a holiday favorite partly because it tackles a problem we all know to be true. Too often, Christmas seems to be all about gifts, decorations, and parties. And

....

Santa Claus, with his bottomless sack of toys, becomes the symbol-in-chief for a month-long shopping fest. As Lucy tells Charlie Brown, "Look, Charlie, let's face it. We all know that Christmas is a big commercial racket. It's run by a big eastern syndicate, you know."

For some people, Santa Claus epitomizes the secularization of modern culture. Most tiny tots with their eyes all aglow spend Christmas Eve wondering about the mystery of flying reindeer, not the mystery of the Nativity. Santa long ago exchanged his bishop's robes and miter for a jolly red suit and pointed cap. Saint Nicholas himself received a blow in 1969 when the Vatican, concluding that his reputation was based more on legend than historical fact, removed him from the ranks of major Catholic saints and made his feast day optional. (In the Eastern Orthodox Church, Nicholas remains one of the most widely venerated saints.)

Some overseas critics resent Santa's popularity. American soldiers began introducing him to foreign lands during the First and Second World Wars. Hollywood movies and television shows helped spread his fame around the globe. In many countries, people adopted him into their Christmas celebrations.

Where Santa Claus has pushed aside local customs,

protests have naturally followed. Small but vocal groups deride him as a purveyor of crass American consumerism, a cheap knock-off of Saint Nicholas. Santa has been burned in effigy before French Sunday-school children. An Anglican vicar once accused him of being a thief who "is stealing the true value of Christmas." Towns in the Netherlands and Belgium have been known to stage mock arrests of Santa Claus and forbid him to appear until after December 6, Saint Nicholas Day. A group of anti-Santa German Catholics has called him "a pack horse of consumer society, nothing more."

What to make of such complaints and criticisms?

One thing is certain. The modern Americanized Saint Nicholas is not going away anytime soon. He is too much a part of the Christmas landscape. He is beloved by hundreds of millions of children and adults. And it is difficult to argue with anything that children love so much.

A wonderful reminder of Santa's goodness came on September 21, 1897, in the pages of the New York *Sun*. Eight-year-old Virginia O'Hanlon had written to the newspaper with a question. "Some of my little friends say there is no Santa Claus," she explained. "Papa says, 'If you see it in *The Sun*, it's so.' Please tell me the truth; is there a Santa Claus?" Francis Pharcellus Church, a former Civil War correspondent, responded in what is perhaps the most famous editorial in the history of American journalism. It read, in part:

Yes, Virginia, there is a Santa Claus. He exists as certainly as love and generosity and devotion exist, and you know that they abound and give to your life its highest beauty and joy. Alas! how dreary would be the world if there were no Santa Claus. It would be as dreary as if there were no Virginias. There would be no childlike faith then, no poetry, no romance to make tolerable this existence. We should have no enjoyment, except in sense and sight. The eternal light with which childhood fills the world would be extinguished.

Not believe in Santa Claus! You might as well not believe in fairies! You might get your papa to hire men to watch in all the chimneys on Christmas Eve to catch Santa Claus, but even if they did not see Santa Claus coming down, what would that prove? Nobody sees Santa Claus, but that is no sign that there is no Santa Claus. The most real things in the world are those that neither children nor men can see. Did you ever see fairies dancing on the lawn? Of course not, but that's no proof that they are not there. Nobody can conceive or imagine all the wonders there are unseen and unseeable in the world. . . .

No Santa Claus! Thank God! he lives, and he lives forever. A thousand years from now, Virginia, nay, ten times ten thousand years from now, he will continue to make glad the heart of childhood.

Yes, Santa Claus is sometimes overexposed and exploited. But anything good is open to being exploited. In fact, anything good is *likely* to be exploited. Such is human nature. Saint Nicholas, in his heyday, was arguably just as overused and overexposed as Santa Claus is today. People called upon him to fulfill every conceivable desire, from finding a husband to conquering an enemy. The citizens of Bari went so far as to steal his bones to give their city a boost.

For that matter, Saint Nicholas was well connected with commerce and materialism long before Santa Claus came along. Many a ship captain prayed to Nicholas for a profitable voyage, many a merchant invoked his name in sealing a lucrative deal. Trade guilds appropriated him in hopes of selling more buttons, barrels, and boots. Hymns proclaimed his power to satisfy: "If anyone place himself before thy painted image, Nicholas, he will have what he wants." Youngsters looked to the kindly bishop for gain. "Saint Nicholas, my good patron, bring me something good!" ran one old French children's song.

There is nothing wrong with exchanging gifts at Christmastime. After all, the Bible tells us that the Magi brought gifts to the baby Jesus. It is when we lose a sense of moderation, when Santa's bag overflows with too many goodies, that the gift-giving and receiving becomes a problem. As the ancient philosophers remind us, there is a proper measure in all things.

It is true that Santa Claus is a secularized version of Saint Nicholas. But that in itself should not turn anyone against the idea of Santa. Just because something is secular does not mean it is bad. The thing we must guard against is emphasizing Santa Claus so much that we minimize Christmas's true meaning. And that is a matter of choice. Again, moderation is the key.

Saint Nicholas was a real man, but as this book stated at its outset, we know almost nothing about him with certainty. So much time has passed, and so many stories have been told about him, that his history has been bound to legend. We read the tales of him saving ships at sea and bringing murdered students to life, and our modern sensibilities tell us they can be no more true than stories of a jolly old fellow who stuffs himself down millions of chimneys every December 24.

Perhaps not literally true. But the stories of Saint Nicholas and Santa Claus are arguably true in a more important way. They are morally true. They offer generosity, kindness, justice, and self-sacrifice over avarice, cruelty, injustice, and self-indulgence. They are about the celebration of human closeness and decency, and the caring for others. They are about families at the hearth. In their totality, they are about the raising of sights and efforts toward a better life.

The image of Saint Nicholas has changed many times through the years. He has always reflected people's longings and needs, whether that be a handful of grain, a safe port in a storm, or a gesture of love. Santa Claus is part of that evolving image. At his best, he stands for virtues that Saint Nicholas champions: compassion, service, selflessness, largeness of spirit.

There is one essential truth in the stories of Nicholas and Santa Claus: the goodness of the gift offered with no expectation of anything in return. The value of three bags tossed through a window in Patara long ago does not lie in the gold they contained. The act of giving and the effects of the act make those bags priceless. That same spirit lives in our time in a parent or other adult who with secret joy watches a wonder-struck child discover on Christmas morning that Santa has paid a nighttime visit.

Santa Claus is, in a very real sense, the result of a Christ-inspired goodness that has rippled across seventeen centuries, from Nicholas's time to our own. Despite secularization and commercialization, Santa Claus is a manifestation of Nicholas's decision to give to others. The history of Saint Nicholas and Santa Claus is a kind of miracle in itself. It is a legacy that resonates with God's love.

So now you know something of who Saint Nicholas was, and of how Santa Claus came to be. Saint Nicholas's bags of gold have become Santa's sack of toys. It is a piece of history worth knowing, especially at Christmastime. May it help us remember the true spirit of Christmas and the message of loving one another brought to us by a babe in a manger so long ago.

Cann, D. L. *Saint Nicholas, Bishop of Myra: The Life and Times of the Original Father Christmas*. Novalis, Toronto, 2002.

An exploration of the world in which Nicholas lived.

Crichton, Robin. *Who Is Santa Claus? The True Story Behind a Living Legend*. Canongate, Edinburgh, 1987.

A history of Saint Nicholas and various customs associated with Christmas.

Ebon, Martin. *Saint Nicholas: Life and Legend*. Harper & Row, New York, 1975.

Nicholas's transformation from bishop of Myra to Santa Claus.

Jones, Charles W. *Saint Nicholas of Myra, Bari, and Manhattan: Biography of a Legend.* University of Chicago Press, Chicago, 1978.

A detailed, scholarly history of the legends and traditions associated with Nicholas.

Seal, Jeremy. *Nicholas: The Epic Journey from Saint to Santa Claus.* Bloomsbury, New York, 2005.

A biographical travelogue tracing the story of Santa Claus from its ancient origins to today.

Wheeler, Joe L., and Jim Rosenthal. *St. Nicholas: A Closer Look at Christmas.* Nelson Reference, Nashville, 2006.

A coffee-table book rich with photographs of Saint Nicholas icons and artifacts.

The Saint Nicholas Center, www.stnicholascenter.org.

A website loaded with information about the story of Saint Nicholas and Saint Nicholas traditions around the world.